20

31

First published in the UK 1999 by St George's Hospital Medical School and Gaskell.

Second edition published 2017 by Books Beyond Words.

Text & illustrations © Books Beyond Words, 2017.

ISBN 978-1-78458-076-6

British Library Cataloguing-in-Publication Data
A catalogue record for this book is available from the British Library.

Printed by DX Imaging, Watford.

Books Beyond Words is a Community Interest Company registered in England and Wales (7557861).

Further information about the Books Beyond Words series can be obtained from Beyond Words' website: www.booksbeyondwords.co.uk.

Contents

Storyline

The following words are provided for readers and supporters who want some ideas about one possible story. Most readers make their own story up from the pictures.

1. Barbara and Janet are chatting.

2. Mike and Harry say, "Hello."

3. Harry knows Barbara. Janet says, "Hello." She does not know Mike.

4. Harry and Barbara are sitting close together. Janet and Mike are getting to know each other.

5. They all think about going to the cinema.

6. They are eating popcorn in the cinema.

7. "Sh-sh!" "Don't spoil the film."

8. The usher tells them to leave. They come out of the cinema. They are upset.

9. The girls are falling in love.

10. Janet wants to ring Mike. She feels shy. Mike wants to phone Janet. Harry says, "Go on."

11. Mike and Janet talk on the phone.

12. Mike comes to Janet's house.

13. Janet and Mike want to be alone. Barbara wants to watch TV.

14. Mike says, "Goodbye." Janet wants him to stay.

15. Janet goes to Mike's house. He opens the door.

16. Janet meets Mike's dad.

17. Dad goes out – now they are alone.

18. Mike and Janet kiss.

19. Mike says, "Come to bed with me."

20. Janet turns away. She says, "No." She doesn't want to go to bed.

21. It is hard to talk. Both feel shy and a bit hurt.

22. Then they talk.

23. They listen to music together.

24. Janet introduces Mike to her mum and dad.

25. Mike and Janet enjoy lots of things together. They walk in the park and go to the seaside. At Christmas they give each other presents.

26. They go window shopping. Mike watches football. Janet looks at wedding dresses.

27. They talk about getting married.

28. Janet's parents are worried. What will happen in the future? "Where will you live?" "What about money?" "And what if you have a baby?"

29. Janet and Barbara talk about things. Janet talks about getting engaged and getting married. They talk about sex, birth control and babies. They wonder where Janet and Mike would live.

30. Mike and Harry talk about the same things.

31. Mike and Janet love each other. They decide to get married.

32. They choose an engagement ring.

33. Mike puts the ring on Janet's finger.

34. They tell Janet's parents.

35. They tell Harry and Barbara.

36. Mike and Janet are happy together.

37. Mike and Janet plan their future.

38. Everyone says, "Congratulations!"

Love

Loving is part of being human, and so is touching and being touched. Sex is a natural part of this, and the part we often find most difficult for ourselves, let alone trying to support anyone else.

People may need practical as well as emotional support about making friends and enjoying close and intimate relationships. This can create unique complications for parents and others who also wish to provide care and protection, but may not like their grown-up children's choices. If their child has a learning disability this can make it harder to allow a 'dignity of risk'. In the wish to protect, parents may be unaware they are stifling normal growth.

Some parents may feel more comfortable than others when discussing personal matters with their son or daughter. Others may find it helpful to talk first to a third party who knows their son or daughter well, if they have any concerns. Most important of all, their son or daughter should be encouraged to speak about these personal things, which they may think are taboo.

Hurt

Relationships can be painful and most of us can remember a time when we felt sad, lonely, angry, scared or lost because a loving relationship had come to an end. This sort of pain is part of being alive and when we try to protect someone, it takes away precious freedoms as well.

All young adults require privacy to develop emotionally and sexually. Where privacy is not provided, important areas of growth are spoilt or distorted. People with learning disabilities should have the chance to make ordinary mistakes, just as we all do. Their reward will be the opportunity to experience joy, excitement and fun as well.

Healthy and appropriate sexual expression should not be restricted, because people who are kept in ignorance are more likely to show disturbed behaviour or to be abused.

Culture and sexuality

This book cannot hope to reflect the wide diversity of lifestyles or religious, ethnic and moral views and choices in our society. Individuals and their families will still need to think the issues through for themselves. It will help if parents and carers have a confident, open and explicit approach to the subject.

Legality, permission and consent – guidelines for support workers and professionals

People often mix up these three concepts, and professionals in particular worry that they may be supporting a relationship that is unsafe, or even against the law. Health and safeguarding are very important. Above all, despite all practical concerns and social taboos, it is important to remember how vital human loving (including sexual love) can be for people's health and happiness.

The most important concept is consent. Consent can sometimes be very complicated – for instance, someone consenting to medical treatment needs to know about side-effects, reasons for treatment and so on. Consent to be in a relationship and to take part in intimate activity should involve an understanding of the emotional and physical effects of intimacy, including risks and benefits. For instance it is important that both participants should understand that sex should be pleasurable for them and that they can say no to any activity at any time. Some people may need visual support, such as the pictures in this book, or in the Beyond Words book *Loving Each Other Safely*, which shows images of safe consensual sexual activity, to support a conversation about these topics. People often demonstrate their consent by their actions rather than in words.

If you can answer 'yes' to all the following questions, then it's likely to be a healthy and safe relationship.

- Do both people in the relationship have learning disabilities?

- Are both people in the relationship able to make decisions and act independently in another area of daily living? Such as:

  » being able to show pleasure in any one activity

  » having clear preferences in diet or in which TV programmes they watch

  » enjoying other social activities such as games and entertainment in company

  » making decisions about what to wear

  » holding a conversation, or using gestures or other body language to communicate

- Has the relationship grown over time?

- Are both people more or less equally active in maintaining contact with each other?

- Do you think there is a reasonable balance of power between the partners?

- Do both people seem to enjoy the relationship?

- Do both people appear happy in their relationship?

- Do both people know about and understand safe sex and contraceptive precautions?

If you answered 'no' to any of these questions, what can you do to reduce any possible harmful effects in the relationship? For example, could one of the partners benefit from learning how to express their needs more clearly?

If you think the situation is more complex or there are some risks that are not easily addressed, there are some more formal tools available to assess capacity to consent to sex. See Useful resources (p.50).

If you do not feel a relationship is safe or healthy, how can you support the partners? It is probably best to engage both people in a dialogue, and bring out any concerns that way.

As with any other activity, staff and carers should:

- Assess and minimise any risks, and maintain their duty of care.

- Help adults with learning disabilities to achieve a good quality of life.

- Encourage them to develop their competence to choose.

- Show respect for their individuality and dignity.

- Follow established safeguarding procedures if they feel that someone they are working with is suffering from, or at risk of, harm or abuse.

Useful resources

Services in the UK

Community Learning Disability Teams (CLDTs)
These are specialist multidisciplinary health teams that support adults with learning disabilities and their families by assessment of their health needs and a range of clinical interventions. Teams may include therapists and psychologists, who can provide specialist intervention to support communication, activities of daily living, and mental health.

Dating services
There are a number of regional dating services specifically for people with learning disabilities. Most offer the opportunity to make new friendships, as well as supported introductions and dates, and events such as speed dating. It is important to check out any service carefully before using it to make sure it is safe and supportive.

Hampshire
Love4Life
www.fitzroy.org/love4life-about
Telephone: 01329 826423

Yorkshire
Luv2MeetU
www.luv2meetu.com
Telephone: 01274 655956

Oxfordshire
Mates 'n' Dates
www.matesndates.org.uk
Telephone: 01933 899980

Scotland
dates-n-mates
www.dates-n-mates.co.uk
Telephone: 0141 427 2957

Brook
Brook is a UK organisation providing information and advice to all young people on issues of sexual health. Local drop in centres offer counselling and support as well as contraception and testing for STIs. Brook also deliver training to teachers and other professionals working with young people.
www.brook.org.uk

Family Planning Association (FPA)
The FPA provide advice, support and resources about sexual health via their website. They also offer a range of training, including courses for families, professionals and people with learning disabilities.
www.fpa.org.uk

Ann Craft Trust (formerly NAPSAC)
Provides advice and training for the caring professions on sexuality and learning disabilities and on sexual abuse.
Telephone: 0115 951 5400
www.anncrafttrust.org

Respond
Respond provides services for young people and adults with learning disabilities who have experienced sexual abuse or who display sexually harmful behaviours. Services include: risk assessments, psychotherapy, prevention and education workshops, training and consultation. Respond also operates a

free helpline for people with learning disabilities, carers and professionals.
www.respond.org.uk
Helpline: 0808 808 0700

Written materials and online resources

Sexual Health and Relationships: A Review of Resources for People with Learning Disabilities. This is a comprehensive review of over 60 different resources on sexual health and relationships for people with learning disabilities. It is available on the **NHS Health Scotland** website:
www.healthscotland.com/documents/1185.aspx

Capacity Assessment for Sex Tool
A **BILD** assessment resource, designed to support professional judgement around capacity, consent and risk issues. The tool can help to identify if a person has capacity to consent to sex, or if they may develop capacity with further education. The assessment can be supported with pictures in the BILD title *Exploring Sexual and Social Understanding* (Dodd et al, 2007), which can be ordered from the BILD website. The assessment can be downloaded free.
www.bild.org.uk/our-services/books/essu

The Specials
This is a web series about relationships between a group of friends with learning disabilities. On their website you can watch the series and access the links to YouTube, Facebook and Twitter.
www.the-specials.com

Related titles in the Books Beyond Words series

Making Friends (2015, 2nd edition) by Sheila Hollins and Terry Roth, illustrated by Beth Webb. Neil wants to get to know someone new. This book shows how he learns when he can and can't touch other people.

Hug Me Touch Me (2015, 2nd edition) by Sheila Hollins and Terry Roth, illustrated by Beth Webb. Janet wants someone to hug her but always picks the wrong person. This book tells how she learns when she can and can't hug and touch people.

Loving Each Other Safely (2011) by Helen Bailey and Jason Upton, illustrated by Catherine Brighton. Getting close to someone in a relationship is exciting and rewarding. But it's important to stay healthy and safe. This book aims to help young men explore their own sexuality, choose what to do in a steady relationship, and know how to stay healthy.

Susan's Growing Up (2001) by Sheila Hollins and Valerie Sinason, illustrated by Catherine Brighton. This story shows how a young girl is helped to cope with her first period by her teacher at school and by her mother.

Speaking Up for Myself (2002) Sheila Hollins, Jackie Downer, Linette Farquarson and Oyepeju Raji, illustrated by Lisa Kopper. Having a learning disability and being from an ethnic minority group can make it hard to get good services. Natalie learns to fix problems by being assertive and getting help from someone she trusts.

George Gets Smart (2001) by Sheila Hollins, Margaret Flynn and Philippa Russell, illustrated by Catherine Brighton. George's life changes when he learns how to keep clean and smart. People no longer avoid being with him and he enjoys the company of his work mates and friends.

Books Beyond Words

A wide range of other titles is available in this series. See www.booksbeyondwords.co.uk.

Authors and artist

Sheila Hollins is Emeritus Professor of Psychiatry of Disability at St George's, University of London, and sits in the House of Lords. She has been President of the Royal College of Psychiatrists, and of the British Medical Association and the College of Occupational Therapists, and chair of the BMA's Board of Science. She is founding editor, author and Executive Chair of Books Beyond Words, and a family carer for her son who has a learning disability.

Wendy Perez is a leading self-advocate, disability activist and consultant. Wendy has worked as a consultant for Paradigm as well as working with the Circles Network and she has been a representative on the local government's Partnership Board.

Adam Abdelnoor is founding Chief Executive for Inaura, the inclusion charity, and a chartered psychologist. His main area of expertise is learning and psychological disability.

Beth Webb is the artist who helped to develop the concept of Books Beyond Words in its early days. She is also the author of 14 novels for children and young people and is a professional storyteller.

Acknowledgments

We would like to thank our editorial advisers, Nigel Hollins and Lloyd Page; the Women's Group and staff at Blakes & Link Employment Agency (Hammersmith & Fulham Social Services); and the Men's Group and staff at Lifecare NHS Trust.

We are grateful to Valerie Sinason and Alice Thacker who gave their time most generously to help us.

Our special thanks to art assistant, Linda Nash.

Beyond Words: publications and training

Books Beyond Words are stories for anyone who finds pictures easier than words. A list of all Beyond Words publications, including print and eBook versions of Books Beyond Words titles, and where to buy them, can be found on our website:

www.booksbeyondwords.co.uk

Workshops for family carers, support workers and professionals about using Books Beyond Words are provided regularly in London, or can be arranged in other localities on request. Self-advocates are welcome. For information about forthcoming workshops see our website or contact us:

email: admin@booksbeyondwords.co.uk

Video clips showing our books being read are also on our website and YouTube channel: www.youtube.com/user/booksbeyondwords and on our DVD, *How to Use Books Beyond Words*.

How to read this book

This is a story for people who find pictures easier to understand than words. It is not necessary to be able to read any words at all.

1. Some people are not used to reading books. Start at the beginning and read the story in each picture. Encourage the reader to hold the book themselves and to turn the pages at their own pace.

2. Whether you are reading the book with one person or with a group, encourage them to tell the story in their own words. You will discover what each person thinks is happening, what they already know, and how they feel. You may think something different is happening in the pictures yourself, but that doesn't matter. Wait to see if their ideas change as the story develops. Don't challenge the reader(s) or suggest their ideas are wrong.

3. Some pictures may be more difficult to understand. It can help to prompt the people you are supporting, for example:

- Who do you think that is?
- What is happening?
- What is he or she doing now?
- How is he or she feeling?
- Do you feel like that? Has it happened to you/ your friend/ your family?

4. You don't have to read the whole book in one sitting. Allow people enough time to follow the pictures at their own pace.

5. Some people will not be able to follow the story, but they may be able to understand some of the pictures. Stay a little longer with the pictures that interest them.

58

Falling in Love

Sheila Hollins, Wendy Perez and Adam Abdelnoor illustrated by Beth Webb

Beyond Words

London